Girl, You Are Golden

12 Lessons about Love, God, and Relationships

Shaquetta Hassell

ISBN: (9780578927275)

Library of Congress Control Number: 2021914621

Author: Shaquetta Hassell

Editor: Dr. Joel Boyce

Cover Design: Justin W Hardin of Damascus Media Inc.

Photo: Ricky Lawrence

Photo: Dexter D. Cohen of Internal Expedition Images Photography

Printed in the United States of America

Visit www.girlyouaregolden.com

For free resources to help you learn more about what it takes to love yourself whole-heartedly.

This book is dedicated to my Mommy, my sister Keia, Peaches, and WSB.

TABLE OF CONTENTS

INTRODUCTION

Hi and thank you for purchasing *Girl, You Are Golden: 12 Lessons about Love, God, and Relationships.* I hope that by reading this book you will be empowered to love God, love yourself, take care of yourself, and stay true to your identity.

It's difficult to be a young, single, Black woman, especially in today's society. You have a lot of goals you want to reach and different pressures put on you, and a lot of times, you second guess yourself. You have academic goals, and you reach them. You have professional goals; while those can be more challenging, you reach them as well. You keep climbing levels, but do you know when to take a break? Do you know how to give yourself grace?

We go hard academically and professionally, and we try to do it in our personal lives, but it doesn't always work. When it comes to personal goals like dating, keeping God first, and just being happy with being you, those goals sometimes seem impossible. You can maintain a couple of them, but it seems like one or two always fall behind.

Everyday, it's a struggle to forgive yourself for your shortcomings and trust your judgement after making mistakes. Know this, you are more than what you don't accomplish. You will achieve more if you just give yourself time. Just be as patient with yourself as you are with the guy who takes 3-5 business days to text back.

I believe that with a little time, kindness, and 12 lessons, you will remember how to love yourself wholeheartedly.

~ ~ ~

Over the past 10 years, I have learned so much. I had a desire to share the lessons that have been impactful in my life. I attended a Historically Black College and University, Norfolk State University, where I obtained my Bachelor's of Science degree in Biology. Later, I went to Old Dominion University and received my Master's of Education degree in Educational Leadership. Yes, I have learned several lessons. I have learned about people. I have learned about navigating life as a single Black woman and dating in today's society. I have been writing poems for 20 years, and much of my work describes the lessons that I have learned about love, God, and relationships.

One of my most important relationships is the one I have with God. I was raised in the church, so I try to remember to keep God first always. Honestly, it's not always easy to do. When everything in the world is trying to get your attention, sometimes, you leave God behind. Lucky for us though, He never leaves us.

Over the last few years, I have learned how to rely on God and put myself first. I have learned how to love and trust myself. I started keeping some of the love I used to give away so freely. Life comes with many triumphs and tribulations. Dating has been especially difficult for me.

I've fallen in love when I really should have fallen back. I've been disappointed because every time I thought I found someone, he found someone else. I've had times where I doubted my capabilities because I kept getting job interviews, but I did not get the job. It's easy to doubt yourself when your plans aren't matching your outcomes.

However, you can trust God to be there and place people around you to support you. There have been times where I looked at everything I was doing wrong and did not give myself credit for what I was doing right. I've had relationships in which I had to decide if I was truly happy or just making the best of a subpar situation. Everytime I had to make a choice, I relied on others to help me figure it out. One day, I realized I was the help I was expecting. I was capable of doing better and living up to the standards I had set for myself. I just had to trust and love myself.

Who's going to love me like me? Nobody. Keith Sweat said something like that in his song, and he was not lying. One of the best decisions I made was to love myself. I mean I really had to learn to LOVE me. That meant accepting that I am not perfect, making time to take care of myself, and putting myself first. You deserve to be loved first and foremost by you.

~ ~ ~

The purpose of this book is to empower young, single, Black women to love God, love themselves, take care of themselves, and stay true to their identity.

In this book, you will learn or remember how to take time for yourself, how to be confident in your successes, and how to avoid being ashamed of your mistakes. As you read, I hope that you take the time to see if your actions are lining up with what it means to love you.

If you don't stop and take the time to love and trust yourself now, you may often feel like you are in a fog. You will constantly be unsure of yourself and your position in your relationships. You don't want to feel like you have to rely one someone else to help guide and direct you in your life. You want to be the one who is confident in calling the shots. You want to be happy with yourself first.

How do you stay true to yourself in a world filled with filters and false appearances? You stay true to yourself by knowing it is better to be you than to be anyone else around you. It is better to be genuine and make choices that make you feel good about yourself.

As you read *Girl, You Are Golden: 12 Lessons about Love, God, and Relationships*, you will remember how to be self-confident and love yourself. You will remember that God pulls you through every battle, and you are as strong as you are beautiful.

So stop now, breathe, and embrace every good thing about you.

Girl, You Are Golden!

With Love,

Shaquetta

CHAPTER 1

WHO HAS YOUR HEART?

I can do all things through Christ who strengthens me.
Phil 4:13 NKJV

A few years ago, I almost dated a close guy friend of mine until we had a conversation about church. We had known each other for a long time, and he was always super sweet, but something was missing. One day, we had a conversation about going to church, and I discovered that was an issue for him. When I found out he had a problem with religion, I had a problem with him. Dating guys who had an issue with religion had seemingly become a trend in my life. While the trend was unintentional, it was consistent. This man, just like many others to whom I had been attracted, had a problem with church.

It was a problem I couldn't understand. I grew up in the church. I was active in the choir, praise dance team, and Vacation

Bible School. You name it, and I was there. As a little girl, I attended church with my sister and cousins. As I got older, my family stopped attending church as frequently, and I started going with my best friend. I was ALWAYS in church, and it wasn't because anyone forced me to go. I was at church because I wanted to be there.

Almost every time I was interested in someone (and I often was), I would find out that he was uninterested in church. Many times, I tried to make it work anyway. I thought that one of two things would happen.

1. I thought I could convince him that my beliefs about God were right.

2. I thought that in the grand scheme of things, this wouldn't matter anyway.

Looking back at that thought process now, I realize that the second option was just me being silly. Back then, I obviously wasn't dating with the intent of marriage because in the grand scheme of marriage, God definitely matters.

Also, I wasn't as convincing as I thought I was. I was the one who was being convinced. When a man would tell me that religion didn't matter and follow up with thoughtfulness and consistency, who was I to tell him that it did matter?

Over the years, it's been a struggle for me to make God a priority in my life. When it came to dating, it seemed like that priority was even more negotiable. I would say that I'm a Christian, and act as if loving the Lord was a standard, but then I end up treating God like an option. How could I truly expect any of those relationships to work when I wasn't putting God first? I wasn't even technically putting myself first because I kept compromising my own standards. While this may seem cheesy, I've always wanted to be a deacon and deaconess in the church with my future husband. However, if that ever was going to even be a possibility, I had to get my love for God straight. I had to decide whether I was going to be with Him, or I wasn't going to be with Him. Choosing to love God meant choosing to make Him a priority in my life. Choosing God as a priority in my life meant I had to choose a man who had that same priority. I no longer could wrestle with the option of settling for loving a man who did not love God.

Your faith is not a standard you should be willing to negotiate. There are a lot of attributes and situations on which we can and will compromise while we are in a relationship, but your spirituality shouldn't be one of them. If you truly love God, then compromising the love you have for Him or the time you share with Him eventually will break your heart.

At your core, you are a woman of God, no matter how close or far you feel from Him during the different stages in your life. Much of who you are and how you operate is determined by your faith, your morals, and the manner in which you were raised. Your faith has to be bigger than the doubts that this world places in you. This world will have you not knowing who God is, doubtful about who you are, and confused about who God is to you.

It is hard to stand firm on your foundation when all around you it is being broken apart. However, Psalms 73:26 says, "My flesh and my heart may fail, but God is the strength of my heart and my portion forever." It is imperative to stand firm on the faith, beliefs, and values that helped you to become the woman you are today. It's okay to listen to others and to have discussions about different beliefs, church, and God. However, it's not okay for anyone to make you feel like you are wrong for believing in God.

There was, of course, another occasion when I went on a date with a guy I had known since college. He was an accomplished and attractive young man, but he also had a problem with church. We sat together for a while and enjoyed each other's company. I listened to him and debated with him about church and religion. I expressed to him the love I had for Jesus and tried to convince him that it was a love we all should have. He told me that he was raised in a different denomination, and he supported wherever people needed to go to receive that "motivation." However, he said church just wasn't "it" for him. It was clear that our beliefs were different, but I had a really hard time dealing with that. He, like many others I knew, was raised in the church. Therefore, it was hard for me to grasp how it was so easy to just denounce the values we were taught. I just felt like people had become too "woke" for their own good, and they needed to fall back asleep.

"Trust in the LORD with all your heart, And lean not on your own understanding" Proverbs 3:5. I had a hard time defining and defending what church and religion meant to me. It's hard to define who God is to you to someone else. However, it's not just about religion. It's about having a relationship with God. When you have a personal relationship with God, it isn't easy to share with others everything God is to you or has been to you. A few years ago, I started hearing this phrase "relationship vs. religion". I didn't understand what it meant then, but I understand it now. I was saved at a very early age, and my love for God is innate, so it has always been a relationship for me. I wasn't just saying prayers or singing songs because it was a tradition. I was praising God because that was what my heart felt.

How do you explain what your heart feels on the first date even if it is about God? It's difficult, and you have to be courageous and intentional. Even though I had no problems asking guys about their beliefs, I had a really hard time accepting that their beliefs were different from my beliefs. Also, proving to them how much God meant to me was a constant battle. However, you shouldn't have to prove to someone who God is to you. You should be able to agree on some basic things, accept each other's beliefs, and decide if a difference in faith is a dealbreaker for you, and it's okay if it is! Remember, your love for God is a major part of your identity. If someone is not in alignment with who you are, there's no need in trying to make him fit because he won't.

It takes courage to put your faith first in a society in which loving God is not always popular. Sometimes, you will struggle and move away from God, but He always loves you. It's funny how things work out in your favor even when the outcome is not what you initially desired. God has a way of working things out for you. Always choose God and prioritize your relationship with Him because He keeps, loves, and protects you. It's okay if you have to tell a man, "No we can't date because we have different values." Don't try to force the relationship or make it work. Don't compromise your faith for a relationship. The relationship that is right for you will not require you to do that.

CHAPTER 2

ADDRESS THE STRESS

Diverged

Luckily in my dreams I found myself surrounded

By lilacs, roses, & lilies

Sweetness replacing the bitterness

I could never seem to escape.

In reality, I endured restless nights contemplating how the path we were on diverged into two roads

Mine leading to a dead end,

with me only looking back for you

and Yours leading to her

with no thoughts of the one you left behind;

Me

Seems like it would always be me who was left behind

because you weren't the first one

Or the last one to leave

And if I knew then

what I know now

I would be able to cleave

Happily

Because God has a way of removing

those who aren't meant to stay

By: Shaquetta Hassell

I've had my heart broken several times over the years, but it wasn't until I experienced a really bad break up that I even considered the idea of going to therapy. I had been before for a short period of time, but I didn't know how helpful it could really be. While therapy is more accepted now, I still felt some shame about going to my sessions. I felt weak. Everybody had break ups, so why was it that my breakup had to send me to therapy? A while later, I finally made the decision to go to therapy. I searched for a Black female therapist and made the appointment. Best. Decision. Of. My. Life. A year had passed since the breakup, so I felt like I was pretty healed from it. The event that finally led me to make the appointment was work. Work has always caused a different type of stress for me. I set my expectations high, and my tolerance is low for the bullcrap. I don't get upset easily; however, when people are being nasty or unprofessional, I can't tolerate it after a certain point. The truth is that although work is the one thing that always drove me to therapy, it wasn't my only issue. Work stress was the icing on the cake, but it didn't taste sweet. Work stress bothered me, but underneath it, there were relationship concerns and personal issues. I tried to hide it, but my heart still had not healed from the break up. When I reflect on the situation now, I'm grateful that the people at work were cutting up. The work situation and stress gave me the push I needed to go get a different type of healing that I didn't know I needed.

Work was the one thing I usually had some control over, and once I felt like it had control over me, I knew it was time to seek extra help. Stress literally can kill you. Many times, as young, single, Black women, we take on a lot. We've become really good at doing a whole lot. Sometimes, we don't realize that we've taken on more than we can handle. Throughout our lives, we have learned and managed to "PUSH THROUGH." However, in the same way that you can run yourself ragged, you can push until you plummet too. It is okay to need support, and more importantly, it's okay to ask for it. Therapy is a tool that will help you to feel like you don't have to push alone. When you have a good therapist, you will feel like you barely have to push at all. You will have someone there to stand with you and help guide you. Your therapist is someone who has your back and is there to catch you if you fall.

Issues at work drove me to therapy, but before that, I had considered therapy after dealing with a stressful breakup. This break up was Earth shattering for me. It was extremely unexpected and drawn-out. The break up started with my ex-boyfriend saying he didn't feel the same way about me anymore. He periodically contacted me and disturbed my peace for months after the breakup, even though he had a whole new relationship.

After we broke up, I felt ashamed. I tolerated too much in our relationship. I felt like I deserved every bad thing that happened to me because I knew better. There were signs and moments in time where I KNEW I should have left him. I felt like the negative things I dealt with as a result of our relationship were because of the things I chose not to deal with when I was still in the relationship.

Even a woman in love is human. Humans make mistakes. I was incredibly hard on myself. I carried a lot of guilt and wasn't very forgiving of myself. Without going to therapy, I don't think I would have recognized that. Someone once told me, "It is not your fault for loving and trusting a man." Although it took some time for me to believe that statement, it is the truth. You may wish that you had not been blind to certain situations. There may be some things you wish you didn't do, or there may be things that you wish didn't happen, but there is no way to reverse time and undo those things. Not forgiving yourself for past events that you could not control is not healthy. It's not what God would want for you, and it's also not what I want for you.

Let's not just walk around feeling bothered but not dealing with it. Stress takes a toll on your body. Heartbreaks hurt, and it's okay to seek help when you realize that months have gone by, and you still are unhappy. When you can't seem to escape feelings of sadness or anger, therapy is a tool you can use to help move you forward. It's easy to stay stuck and not share your feelings. Try not to blame yourself for the pain that others caused you.

It is difficult, but it is doable. You are not responsible for the terrible way you were treated. Your only job now is to pray and ask God to continue to help you do whatever it takes to help you heal.

CHAPTER 3

IS GOD ON THE CALENDAR?

God please give me peace.
Give me Your peace.
And in the moments where I have peace,
Please don't allow anything to disturb it.
Amen.
By: Shaquetta Hassell

2020 proved to be one heck of a year. At the top of the year, I was really excited about my upcoming birthday in March and my plans to visit California for the first time. I had everything ready, from the activities, to the outfits, to the shoes. I had purchased my flight back in November, but on Friday, March 13, the world as we knew it changed. The world basically shut down, and nothing was the same. The virus came and put a fear in a lot of people, but I did not have those same fears. I wasn't being reckless, but perhaps, I was being a little selfish. Birthdays are always a big thing for me, and I had been prepping for this trip for months. The last thing I wanted to do was cancel it. When my friends started asking questions in the group chat, and I saw the news reports about travel bans, I started getting frustrated. I had no intention of canceling my plans, but as the situation rapidly developed, I had no choice but to cancel my flight 2 days before the birthday trip. I could not risk taking a trip and not being able to come back home.

I had plans, but God had different ones. I'm sure many of us can relate to this in general but especially over the last year. While I was unable to go on my birthday trip, I had some fun alternate plans with my girlfriends. We were able to do a fancy dinner right before the restaurants shut down, and we had a slumber party to bring in my birthday at midnight. It actually turned out to be one of the best birthdays I had. I was so caught up in how I wanted things to go that I didn't stop and just be thankful for what I had. I was so laser focused on my original plans, that I wasn't open to anything else. Canceling my trip and dealing with the pandemic reminded me how I ought to be when things don't go my way. I have to be a little more flexible and always grateful. Birthdays are big to me because you literally would not be here without them. However, with a year like 2020, I was definitely grateful to God just to be able to see another birthday.

As I've said before, sometimes, I struggle with making God a priority. I love and trust God, but I don't always set aside time for Him. As a child, going to church was all I knew. It was all my social activities, but as a young adult, there is so much more to do including parties, friends, family, and guys. Sometimes it's just hard to put God on the schedule.

God was never meant to be second. God deserves not just some of our time, but He deserves to be prioritized. Each day, God strengthens you. He restores you. He renews our hope in a world that drains us all. There have been times in my life when I can look back and see how God literally carried me through situations. I had no will of my own to do it. Who are we not to set aside time for God and simply say, "Thank You"? We should take time to pray, read a Bible verse of the day, and/or do a quick devotional. Prayer doesn't have to be a super official, long, or thought-out speech to God. We can thank God for waking us up in the morning. You can talk to Him during the day or pray to Him when your coworker is talking to you crazy. Prayer is a meaningful and simple way to spend time with God. It's a straightforward way to thank God and ask Him for the things you need. It is easy to remember to pray when we are going through it, but we have to make a more conscious effort to pray when times are good or bad.

My senior year in college was a tough year for me. Despite the fact that I had all my "easy" classes, it was difficult balancing my senior needs versus my senior wants. One of the major things I needed to do that I neglected to do was to make a decision about my post graduate plans. I waited until senior year to make a final decision about what I was going to do after college. I wasn't sure which route I wanted to take careerwise anymore. All my life, I wanted to be a doctor, but when senior year hit, I wasn't sure if my next step was going to be medical school, another professional school, or teaching.

I was torn about what to do because I honestly wasn't looking forward to the next steps that came after graduation. I wasn't excited about attending medical school. I wasn't even looking forward to the steps I had to take to apply to medical school. I sought advice from teachers, advisors, friends, and those who had graduated before me. I had an older friend tell me that although medical school would be extremely stressful, it would be worth it. My teachers told me that I would be great at whatever I chose to do. One of my advisors said that I was too smart to teach, and I needed to go to medical school or another professional school.

So I did. I chose to go to graduate school. For one semester, I almost drowned from the stress and workload of being in a very rigorous graduate program. I cried daily. On the Fourth of July, I was in class. I studied endlessly but still failed my exams. I struggled with relating to my teachers and classmates, and ultimately, I failed one of my classes. I was the only Black woman in my cohort. I had never failed a class before in my life. The embarrassment was real, and I felt defeated. I chose something haphazardly. Going to graduate school sounded good, but it wasn't what I truly wanted to do. I wish I would have taken more time to figure out what I wanted to do. I wish I had cared less about what others thought of me if I took a break or decided to teach.

God will allow you to go in the wrong direction. He will allow you to make your own choices and mistakes. When you procrastinate on decision making and choose not to include God in your planning, don't be surprised if you are met with disaster.

You have to set time aside to include God in your plans and your planning. When you need advice on an outfit, you spend time looking in the mirror, pairing different shoes with it, and possibly Facetiming your best friend to get her input. What if we spent that same time asking God to help us in our decision making? How much better would your plans turn out if you made time to share them with God like you do with everyone else?

Relationships require time. You make time for the people in your life like your mom, sister, friends, and boyfriend. You enjoy spending time with them and appreciate the time they share with you. When you pray, read the Bible, or simply sit still, you allow God to ease your thoughts and reassure you. We make time for all our other relationships and obligations, so it can't be that hard to make time for God. All that you have and all that you have accomplished are gifts from God. Spend time with Him, so you will remain grateful and humble. Spend time with God, so you are able to take on the sunshine and the storms.

First and foremost, God. Let's try to put Him first. Acknowledge how good He has been to you and how He is there in your times of need. God supplies every blessing. We become so busy with life that sometimes we forget the smallest things like a thank you to God. This is actually one of the most important things we should be doing. When you fall off, just get back on it. Do what you can and pray. Remember the times God showed up for you and surround yourself with people who support your spiritual growth.

Chapter 4

Select All That Apply

Go confidently in the direction of your dreams! Live the life you have imagined.- Henry David Thoreau

For years, I had been writing poems and not really doing anything with them. I was afraid to recite my poems or post them on social media because I feared what other people would think, if I shared them. I have been writing poems since I was 10 years old. Over the years, when I did share my poems, people usually would say they were good, but sad. After reciting a poem to a friend one time, she asked me, "Girl, are you okay?" I was fine, but her question bothered me. I was reciting a poem that was written years ago. Yes, it was sad, but what heartbreak isn't sad? As I've gotten older, I've realized that I wrote a lot of poems when I was going through something. Poetry was kind of like therapy for me. I had to accept the fact that I couldn't please everybody with my words.

It was okay for me to write poems that were sorrowful. My words were not for them; they were for me. They were also for people who could relate to what I was experiencing. After a while, I jokingly started calling myself the Mary J. Blige of poetry. I wrote poems about a lot of different topics: God, sex, food, math, and love. However, the poems I wrote about being heartbroken were some of my best ones.

I made a choice that changed my life. I decided to stop entertaining the thought of considering what others thought of me, and I recited my poetry on an Instagram live event. You will spend a lot of time and energy thinking about what other people think of your choices if you allow yourself to do that. It is not easy to ignore what everyone else thinks, but at times, it is necessary. Fear and outside opinions will prevent you from pursuing your passions. It is scary to make a decision all by yourself, but you have to be confident in your selections. You know what's best for you, and you also know what you can handle. You know what you can tolerate. You may ask others for advice when you are going through a situation. However, you are the ONLY one who has to live with that decision in your life. Even if others are affected by your choices, a decision that you make for yourself is going to "hit different" for them. It's not going to affect them the same way because they don't have to live your life.

Reciting my poems on Instagram live was the absolute BEST time of my life. I felt confident, sexy, and empowered. I did not tell many people about the live event; in fact, I only told about 5 of my friends shortly before it started. I didn't tell them because I was afraid I might mess up. I also just thought about keeping it to myself. I was confident in the knowledge that I had chosen to do something by myself, for myself. I also didn't tell my friends because I didn't want to be asked too many questions. Sometimes, questions promote doubt. Being asked a lot of questions about my plans makes me feel like I am defending myself about my choices.

I had no room for any doubts to be placed in my head about what I was going to do. If you are about to do something BIG, you don't want to feel like you're on the defense. All you want to feel is support and encouragement, and you deserve that. This is why you sometimes have to do things alone. You have to make your own choices. This doesn't mean you can't call on family or friends for support, but you alone have to take the first step. You may be alone in the beginning or at the end, but that doesn't mean you will be alone for the whole process. Be confident in the knowledge that your choices are good choices for you. Those who love you will be there to support you. There is no more room for doubts. You need to walk confidently in the direction that you choose for your life.

Don't be afraid of taking new steps. Put yourself out there. In your heart, you know what you truly want to do, but you just have to find the courage to do it. You might find that the risk is worth the reward. Be confident in your choices and actions. Don't be surprised if that thing you were afraid to do actually works out. It is empowering to explore new options and ways to be creative.

Know that as you choose what is right for you, you can't please everyone. You should not try to please everyone either because it simply won't work. Do what works for you.

CHAPTER 5

GOAL-GETTER

Independent - She chooses her own path and does what works for her. She is not persuaded by the opinions of others.

When I date, my end goal is marriage, so I try to pace myself accordingly, but I haven't always been successful at that. There was a time in my life when I made marriage the middle goal as well. I did some things wrong when I treated a boyfriend like a husband. I am SO glad that even during that time, I still had some goals I wanted us to pursue independently before we pursued them collectively. One of the major goals I had for myself was to purchase my own home.

After dating a man for about 6 months, he was ready to move in together and purchase a home. I was not with it. In fact, I encouraged him to proceed without me. We weren't in the position to rush and get married just for the purpose of purchasing a home.

For me, I had a dream as a bachelorette to buy my own house. I wanted to see how it would be to live by myself before I decided to merge my life with someone else and create a home together. I felt like that was something that was not only okay for us to do individually, but also it was needed. It is important to establish your routines, likes, and dislikes for managing your home before creating a home with someone else. Personally, I had a goal of waiting until I was married before living with someone. I know this may seem very old-fashioned and ridiculous to some people, but it was my goal. While I can see the value of living with your love, I feel like in today's society, there isn't much that separates long-term relationships from marriage.

Most of us are having sex in our relationships. Some of us already may have children together, and if we decide to live with our significant other, what is the difference between being a girlfriend and being a wife? What separates dating and marriage if we are already doing everything like we are married? I don't say this as if any of those circumstances are wrong; you must do what works for you. However, I do want to encourage you to do just that. For me, I had a goal of waiting to live with someone until marriage. I had to sit down with my boyfriend at the time and explain to him that it was non-negotiable for me. Even if it didn't make sense to him, it was extremely important that I followed my dream. I wanted to wait until we were married to live together, and I wanted to buy my own dream home by myself, at least the first one.

Be courageous in the goals you pursue. Sometimes, people judge you based on the goals that you have because your goals don't make sense to them. Your goals may seem too big or too small to them. Your goals may not seem realistic or relatable to them. However, remember they are YOUR goals and not their goals. Don't let other people judge you or scare you out of pursuing one of your goals. While my goal for my relationship may seem tiny, it was huge for me. I had to look the person I loved in the eye and see that he didn't understand the path I wanted to choose for myself and our relationship. Whether it be a relationship goal, a career goal, or a personal goal, sometimes, people won't understand the goals you choose to pursue.

I was teaching for a few years before deciding to get my master's degree. When I started the program, I was in a relationship, and when I ended the program, I was single. I was actually in my last summer semester when I was on a rollercoaster ride of breaking up and getting back together with my ex-boyfriend. Ultimately, we broke up, and I was brokenhearted. I never cried so much. I was dejected and lost my motivation for doing my school work. My ex-boyfriend was one of the reasons why I chose to pursue a second degree. He was one of the people who had encouraged me to do it. I had planned for him to be at my graduation. However, right before I was about to cross the finish line, everything changed for the worse. He stopped talking to me. I would go hours without hearing from him, and even when we were together, he didn't have much to say. We weren't arguing, but I knew something was wrong. He started acting differently towards me. Suddenly, he told me his feelings for me had changed, and we were no longer going to be together.

Somehow, I managed to push through and go to my class each day. It was difficult, and I did not want to be there. Everyone could tell there was something wrong with me. One day, one of my classmates asked me if I was okay, and I broke down and cried. I told her almost everything, and although it wasn't my intention to tell her anything, I thank God that she was there. We went out to dinner later that day, and she gave me so much encouragement. In those moments, she helped me to remember my worth. Just because my relationship failed did not mean I had to fail too. It did not mean I had to fail at my dreams. My goals were still valuable.

You are still worthy and capable of achieving your goals even when things fail around you. When awful things happen to you unexpectedly, you still have to see it through. Sometimes, the situation changes, but the goal does not. When life seems to turn on you, it may be easy to give up on your goals, but it will not be fruitful. You will end up with more regrets than accomplishments if you give up. Life is challenging, and it can distract you from your goals but just see it through.

CHAPTER 6

WHAT IF YOU FUMBLE?

Sister

I was crying and could not see the sun through the rain
Then you came
And wiped my tears away.
You wrapped me in your arms
and told me I would be okay
You told me that you know that sometimes it's hard to try
Because we fear that we may fail
You told me you know sometimes it's hard to live
Because we fear that we may die
You told me that sometimes it's even hard to cry
Because we fear telling people why we are aching inside
But the most important thing you told me
Was not to fear
Because you will always be by my side.
By: Shaquetta Hassell

My sister always has encouraged me. Whenever I needed advice or had doubts about my plans, she's been there to reassure me that I was moving in the right direction. As a teacher, I've faced a lot of opposition at work from students, staff, and parents. However, because I love the kids, I always do whatever I can to help them be successful. One year, I decided to create a parent and teacher tutoring night. The night was designed to show parents how the content was taught and how they can better assist their children at home. Students also attended the event, so both the parents and students could review the strategies and material at the same time.

My goal was to prepare the parents to help their children study at home for an upcoming math test. When I tried to implement the plan in my school, I did not get the support I needed, so I decided that I wasn't going to do the event. At that point, I wasn't even sure if I could do it. I questioned if I knew what I was doing at all. Although I wanted to cancel it, something told me to keep trying. I had shared my hopes and frustrations with my friends. The beauty in verbalizing your plans is that it holds you accountable. I wasn't sure if I was making the right choice in spending my own money and proceeding with the event. However, I knew something good would come from the process even if it wasn't being fully supported.

Ask for the support you need. When I didn't get the response I expected from my job, I found another route. I was blessed to have a community sponsor provide food for the event. A few of my friends donated money for the tutoring night. My mentor donated her time and money by running errands for me. Two of my colleagues stayed after school to assist with tutoring the students and parents. The night ended up being a huge success with not only parents and students who attended the event but also with grandmas, siblings, uncles, and aunts.

In life, sometimes, there is more than one right choice. There is even more than one best choice. For example, it was the right thing for me to follow the protocols for creating events at the school. However, that option didn't pan out. As a result, I could have chosen to postpone the tutoring event until my plans were approved, or I could have partnered with another organization, so my idea could come to fruition. Those would have been acceptable choices as well, but I chose a different option.

Be okay with the possibility of making a mistake. As you continue on this journey where you are overcoming setbacks and setting new goals, it may be confusing when you are choosing the road you want to take. Keep in mind that sometimes, there is more than one path that you can take. There is more than one path that may be right for you. The goal is to choose a path that makes you feel comfortable and confident. Choosing a comfortable path means you like where you are headed. You feel comfortable about your next steps, but that doesn't mean you won't be challenged. You feel confident about your path, yet you understand you still will have to work extremely hard. Our fear of failing sometimes prevents us from even trying. So what if you fail? So what if you fumble? There is a success in making the effort. Don't be afraid to try and don't be afraid of making a mistake. There are people wishing for the opportunities you are afraid to take.

You will not be the first person or the last person to try something new and be unsuccessful. You have to trust yourself when you are deciding which path to take. The path you choose may be different from the path that your mother, sister, or best friend will take, but ultimately, the path you choose is yours to take. Don't let the fear of a fumble stop you from setting fire to a new path.

When I graduated from college, I was really excited about becoming a doctor. I chose not to go to medical school, but I attended a graduate school where I studied to be a Doctor of Physical Therapy. As I stated earlier, when I made this shortcut postgraduate plan, God was not exactly included. After watching Common and Queen Latifah on *Just Wright* and seeing that blessing, I just assumed that God supported my plans. I was still becoming a doctor, just in a different field. I saw how much Leslie (Queen Latifah's character) loved the field and how she fell in love, and I fell in love as well. However, I didn't seek God's guidance or pray about the decision. I chose to go to physical therapy school because I had the qualifications, and it seemed less stressful than medical school. Watching *Just Wright* made me feel like physical therapy was the right option for me. I felt that it was an easier path with a similar outcome. I don't think I made a terrible decision, but I could have made a better one. I didn't choose my career path based on passion or prayer. I chose it because of its status and its feasibility. I chose to go to that school because it looked and sounded good, and in the end, I failed.

It was one of the worst summers of my life. I was in class and the cadaver lab for more than 12 hours a day. I was pulling 18 hour days because I would study at home after leaving the lab at night. I didn't really get to see my friends or my family at all. I put my all into my class, and my average steadily progressed, but I was still struggling in school. My first test score was a 17.

By the end of the semester, I was passing quizzes and making 60s on my exams. I thought it was a great improvement, but apparently, it was not good enough. In that program, if you failed one class, you failed out of the entire program, but you could make an appeal. Obviously, I failed the class, but I was sure that I would be granted a chance to start over. However, I was not given another chance, and my appeal was denied.

The pain I felt from that experience was excruciating and lasted for months. I was embarrassed and disappointed in myself. Before that summer, I had never failed a class. I could not understand why God would allow me to fail, even though I gave it my all. Nevertheless, I learned a valuable lesson from that failure. When it comes to making choices for your life, follow your heart and trust God. Never let others deter you from choosing the right path for you.

I made a decision out of fear. I was worried about what other people would think if I did not do some version of what I always said I would do. How do you know when to go against the grain? You go against the grain when your happiness means more than the approval of others. When you evaluate your life, you must decide that you don't have to live up to the expectations that others have for you. The beauty about sharing your goals with others is that they give you support and hold you accountable. The burden of sharing your goals is that you may have to tolerate everyone's opinion at a time when you are trying to figure things out. Please remember that while you may invite some opinions, and tolerate others, you don't have to succumb to anyone's opinion but your own. Another burden about sharing your goals is that sometimes, people hold you too accountable. People don't allot room for growth or a change of plans. Many of us can relate to choosing a major in college that we are not using right now. We have heard the jokes and criticism behind that as well. We may have set goals when we were younger, but as we learned more about them and ourselves, we changed our minds about those goals. You are indeed entitled to change your mind. When you are choosing the road you want to take, don't be afraid of the possibility of making a u-turn. You may decide that while your choice might not be popular, it's the option you are willing to accept at this point in your life. For example, I was at a job where I began to dread going to work. I wanted to leave, but I also was hesitant about what I would encounter at a new job. Starting a new job meant starting all over. I had to learn the people and the culture of a new place. When I made the change, I did not know how it would be. Would I actually choose a better job or would I end up right back where I started? This was a risk I was willing to take because for me, it wasn't just easier to stay where I was.

When I reflect on my past decisions, there are a few times that I always wonder what if? What if I would have followed my dreams and gone to medical school like I had always planned? I was so afraid of failing at that, but I ended up failing anyway. I didn't even try to take the MCAT. Maybe if I would have taken that first step, I would have had an idea if I could get into medical school or not.

When I failed out of graduate school, it was a different type of fumble because I actually tried. I tried my best in school, but it didn't work out. I'm okay with that. I'm okay because I know how much work I put into that endeavor. I never tried to go to medical school, and now I'll never know what the outcome could have been.

Don't be so afraid of failing that you don't even try to achieve a goal you've always wanted. Don't get in your own way! This is why I am so grateful to my sister, my mom, and my friends who encourage me daily. You need accountability partners in your life. You need people who won't let you stop trying. When you go after a new goal, start a new business, or even open yourself up to love, you don't know what the outcome will be. However, if you don't move past the fear of failure, you won't ever know what could have been.

CHAPTER 7

SHINE LIKE THE SUN

Girl, You Are Golden

Girl, You Are Golden

You shine just like the sun,

And someday

Yes I'm hoping one day

You will be someone's sun

Because you glow

You bring brightness to life

Look at how you rise

Even after all of the strife

Even when people don't see your value

I do

You are cinnamon, chocolate, honey delight

You are coconut, lavendar, and olive oil

Sweetness and Strength

And your soul

Knows your soil

But they would never know this

Because Girl, You are Gold

Your beauty brings tears to my eyes

Even when you are not at your best,

You are the most beautiful surprise

You still take the world by surprise

Someday

Yes, I'm hoping one day

You will be someone's sun

And I see you looking for

#relationshipgoals with

Somebody's Son

Just remember girl, before him

You were,

You are,

Someone

Girl, You are Golden

Everything that glitters, Ain't Gold

But You Are

You are fierce, you are real

You are like that morning star

Just like the Sun

You are Lit

You are it

You are everything to God

Look at you

So beautiful

Just as precious as Gold

The crown of a Queen

God made you, so you are already whole

Girl, I pray that you never feel broken

That your glitter never be stolen

You are filled with love, laughs, and confidence,

Girl, You are Golden

By: Shaquetta Hassell

As a little girl, my Mom, my sister, and I would always dress up for the holidays. This was a tradition for us, especially on Thanksgiving, Christmas, and New Year's Eve. We would be all dressed up to go nowhere. We would be showered and smell good, and we would stay in the house. On the morning of New Year's Eve, Mommy would tell us to make sure our outfits were ready to watch the ball drop. Bringing in the new year the right way didn't just mean collard greens, fried chicken, and black-eyed peas. It also meant getting dolled up! At first, I didn't get it. Why did we get dressed up and put on our best clothes if no one was going to see us? My godmother used to say, "Whatever you are doing at midnight is what you will be doing for the rest of the year." I learned that by getting dressed up, I was setting a tone and a standard for my year. I was making myself feel good. Feeling and looking good is important.

I remember one year, I picked my favorite outfit which was a black and white polka dot fluffy skirt with a white top and black cardigan. The skirt had a hot pink waist belt with a big, black heart that connected in the middle of it. I just knew I looked good. My mom told me she didn't know what I was doing wearing a "springtime" skirt in the winter. She said, "So are you just going to be dressing backwards all year then?" I was weak because that definitely wasn't my intention. I just felt pretty and confident in an outfit that looked good on me.

When 2020 hit, and I had to spend birthdays and holidays at home, I was disappointed, but I was ready. I knew how to get dressed up and make myself feel gorgeous, even at home. I carried the values my Mom had instilled in me as a little girl. Life is busy, but sometimes, you have to make time for yourself. Many of us go day to day doing mundane tasks and putting time and energy into everyone but ourselves. On a birthday, you deserve to buy a new dress, get your nails and feet done, get your "hair did," and do your makeup. Sometimes, especially as a woman, looking good helps you to feel good. When you are dressed up, it reminds you of who you are and who you have the potential to be. You are a showstopper, on and off the court. The problem is we don't know how to turn things off.

Take time for yourself. Make a plan. Plan a movie night at the house or with your girls. Make the time to spend a little extra time on you. Put on a cute outfit just because you can. Turn your phone on silent and set it away from you for a few hours to take a mental break from the craziness of the world. Do things to make you feel good. Put yourself first.

On Fridays, I relax. It's the end of the work week, and I take the time to acknowledge and congratulate myself for making it through another week. On Friday nights, I don't cook, clean, or check an email. I grab a nice takeout dinner, come home, turn on a movie, and if I'm in the mood, I might have a glass of wine or a nice hot apple cider. Now, this doesn't mean that every week is difficult. However, I work hard for 40 plus hours outside my home for 5 days a week. What this means is that at the end of the week, I deserve a break, and you deserve a break too!

Don't allow anyone to make you feel bad for taking a break either. You have to take time off to regain your focus and recharge. You deserve to take time off for every time you put in extra hours and did not get paid. You deserve to rest because of how you take care of everyone in your family and show up for your friends in their times of need. Trust me, if you don't take time to take care of yourself, you will find yourself broken down. You will be emotionally, physically, and mentally drained if you don't make time for some self-care. Some of us struggle with taking time for ourselves but start with something really small like taking a nap or a day off.

Self-care is a hobby. It can be done in the form of a massage on your birthday once a year or once every few months. Self-care does not have to be something overly thought-out or extravagant. You can choose a random night and find some cute, sexy pajamas to wear to sleep. After a stressful day, light some candles and play music while taking a long shower or hot bath. You can go shopping and pick up a new pair of shoes or accessories when the seasons change. It's okay to treat yourself. Self-care is reserving time for yourself. Taking care of yourself also means taking care of your physical and mental health. When you take time off from work, schedule a doctor's appointment or go to therapy. That is self-care too.

If you want to feel beautiful from the inside out, take some time to relax. Set aside time at least once a week or twice a month, if not more, to decompress from the stresses of life. I once read somewhere that you should do something that makes you smile or makes you happy every day. I know that may be hard to do every day, but perhaps, you can try to do something for yourself weekly. It's important to take time to do things that make you feel like yourself. If you don't pour into yourself first, it will be very difficult to do any other tasks at home, work, or in your relationships.

Self-care is a form of love. Do you love yourself? Do you show love to yourself? Love yourself by setting aside time to rejuvenate. Love yourself by taking mental breaks and doing things that bring you joy. Although I talk a lot about the extra things you can do to pamper yourself, don't forget the basic things too. Don't forget to do the essentials so that you can take care of yourself. Get good sleep, eat well, and take care of your body. There is only one you. Everyday isn't wonderful, but everyday, you find a way to do what you have to do. This means you deserve a day when you can do whatever you want to do. Choose days for you. Choose days when you get to dress up, feel pretty, and not think about the things that stress you out. You just have to stop sometimes and take a break. As I said in Chapter 2, in the same way that you can run yourself ragged, you can push yourself until you plummet. Give yourself time to take care of your physical and mental health. Make sure you are reserving time just for you.

CHAPTER 8

WHO ELSE CAN YOU BE?

I will praise You, for I am fearfully and wonderfully made; Marvelous are Your works, And that my soul knows very well. Psalms 139:14 NKJV

I've always wanted to teach. It's a part of who I am. I remember being a little girl and creating a computer from my picture dictionary, so I could teach my stuffed animals. I guess I was preparing myself for virtual learning even back then. I love to teach because I love learning. I love sharing what I know with others. Math and Spanish have been two of my love languages for a very long time. This year, I was able to use them both in my classroom and at my school. One day, I was called to the office to help translate for some parents who only spoke Spanish. Although I am not quite fluent yet, with what I did know and with the help of Google Translate (by both parties), we communicated. I got those parents the information they needed. It brought me joy to be able to help those parents. My new work friends looked at me in awe, but I was just doing what I was supposed to do. I love helping others and being friendly and using my resources to assist those around me.

There have been times, however, when I felt like being me has failed me. I tried to help people out, and I was straight up played. I've trusted people who I've known for years, and they turned out to be sheisty instead of supportive. I've been criticized for always smiling and being open. I was told, "This is why people act the way they do towards you." I assume they thought because I was a sweet person they could take advantage of me. They thought that because I was always smiling, they could talk to me any type of way and get away with it. People have told lies about me, and I couldn't figure out why they felt the need to do that. However, here's the thing, people ain't shit! They see in you what they can't dream of finding in themselves, and they treat you poorly because of it. It's a form of bullying. Some people may be jealous of the things you have to offer. They envy the way others are attracted to your joy and spirit. It's hard for them to appreciate their own differences, so it's easier for them to treat you badly because of who you are. Some people are also just manipulative. I began to recognize that while I needed to switch up how I interacted with certain people, the goodness in me was not a problem. When I saw I was being taken advantage of or underestimated, I had to put my foot down. I called people out for their actions. I stopped being as giving towards them because it was taking away from me. I was being drained.

Going through these uncomfortable situations made me wonder, *If I was different, would this not be happening to me?* Maybe, if I smiled less or was less friendly, I wouldn't have to deal with people being ignorant towards me, but some people are just mean. They are rude, they are nasty, and insecure, and there isn't much you can do about that. I wanted the negative things to stop, but I can't change people. People are who they are. Some people are just dumb! They make senseless comments and have no regard for how their actions might make others feel.

Don't change who you are because others cannot see your value. There is literally no one like you. Your smile, your beauty, and your style are unique to you. The way you communicate and even the way you choose not to communicate is specific to who you are as a person. You are a gift, and your characteristics make you the woman you are. You have to remember that a gift is not meant for everybody. Some people are not meant to receive it. They are not open or ready to receive it. It is not terrible to be loving, approachable, reserved, shy, analytical, or strong. Please, don't allow others to make you feel flawed for the characteristics that make you, you. Many of us go through life struggling with who we are and comparing ourselves to others. It's okay to be you! I'm really not sure who else you can be.

This year has been difficult for all of us. Some of us have lost loved ones, had financial hardships, or been unable to see family members. Celebrations and funerals have changed. We just miss people. We miss being able to be around people like we used to be before COVID-19. This year at my job, I met a few really nice people who always tried to make me feel at home.

One of them had a birthday coming up. I found out the day before his birthday that he would be working on his birthday. His only request was a visit from me. He missed having people in the building. I did not have to go into the building to work that day, but I made it my business to go see him on his birthday. I brought him a little birthday lunch, and we sat and talked.

During our conversation we talked about the type of person he was. He was always sweet and welcoming, and he was a gentleman towards me. He told me how there was a time when an old coworker had mistaken his friendliness for something more than what he intended to communicate to her. I could relate. However, what I liked about my friend is that when those instances occurred, he apologized for the misunderstanding, but he explained that being caring was just a part of who he is.

As a man, he was going to offer to help a woman carry her belongings if she had a heavy load. He was going to offer to buy lunch and open doors, and it wasn't because he liked her. It was because being a gentleman was who he was. Now, of course, he would correct anyone who mistook his kindness for interest. In that situation, he moved differently, so things wouldn't become awkward, but in general, he didn't change who he was because of what others might think.

So many times, people have gauged your actions and your personality without really knowing who you are. We have a responsibility to be authentic, but you cannot be authentic if you are always trying to adjust who you are for others. We often adjust who we are and how we look for social media. Social media doesn't make it easy to be your authentic self. It's truly a blessing and a curse. It connects us with friends, family, and strangers across the world. However, it's often a way to waste time, not to mention, it is a way that we keep comparing ourselves to others. Remember this, your standards for beauty and success do not need approval by people on social media. Also remember, the best part of social media is that it allows you to show people what you *want* them to see. When you are looking and comparing yourself to the IG models, you don't know if what they are showing you is *real*. Why would you want to try to live up to an image of something that may not exist?

People can be overly critical about the way you move and shake, so you have to ask yourself, "Am I moving for me or for them?" You decide who you want to be. Whoever that may be, I hope it's someone who is good-hearted and genuine. You should not be adjusting your characteristics to get the approval of others. Each of us is very special and different. Those who love us, know that and appreciate our differences. Don't allow people to make you feel bad about who you are. You have positive characteristic traits that are gifts, which are unique to you. Try not to allow negative people or negative experiences to make you feel bad about the positive characteristic traits that you have.

Be you. Be yourself in every sense of those two words. Don't be ashamed of your body. Don't be ashamed that you talk too much or don't be ashamed of how intelligent you are. Don't dim your light for others. It's hard not to compare yourself to others, but that can be detrimental to your happiness. God made you to be you, not anyone else. Part of loving yourself is accepting who you are. You may have flaws, but remember, we all do.

Some of our flaws can be changed, and they will be changed as we learn and grow. Some of our flaws are things that we have to deal with, and we must realize that we are not "less than" because of them. Remember, you can't change people. It is not your responsibility to be a woman who is liked by everyone. Your only responsibilities are to be genuine, protect your heart, and love yourself.

CHAPTER 9

THE PEOPLE WHO POUR

The People Who Pour

When I don't know I need to be filled

You give me strength,

Compliments,

Encouragement.

I can always rely on you

to be you

And you to fill me

without even realizing I needed to be filled.

You are the People Who Pour;

The people who pour into me

You are the ones I see

When the world has blinded and rejected me

It is you who has protected me.

You are the friends who never neglected me.

You are the family who has accepted me.

You are the sisters who have directed me.

The ones who gave me my next step,

When I was stuck on my last.

The ones who have reminded me

that I am not my past.

You are the people who pour

The people who pour into my life

The people who are in my life.

You are the people who pour.

You've been a cup for me,

More than enough for me.

And God knew

to give me you

All of you,

All you who, are the people that pour

From your full cups

and never empty words

from your smiles,

your jokes,

and your prayers unheard

You are the people who pour.

Better than a dream team.

You are a supreme stream

Of light, love, and so much more.

You are

The people who pour.

By: Shaquetta Hassell

One of my creative girlfriends had been telling me for months, "Girl, you need to go live." Although I'm not the shy type, when it came to doing a live event on social media, I was not feeling it. I was hesitant. First of all, what was I going to say? Secondly, who was going to be up there? I follow many people on social media, and when they go live, I usually pop in to support them and see what's happening. I always wonder what it feels like though, when you go live, and there are only three people up there. I'll be on my phone thinking, *What was the point?* However, one day, I finally said yes to her. It was after I had already done my first live event. The first time I was on IG live, someone invited me to recite a poem for his spoken word night. The second time I went live, my creative girlfriend and I did it together. I told her I wouldn't do it without her, and we ended up planning a whole event. We created a flyer and came up with a theme. We did promo for a week and even did a couple of run throughs before the actual event. The best part was that we had more than three people attend our event. It turned out to be an amazing event.

Without my girlfriend constantly checking in on me and pushing me to step out of my comfort zone, I never would have done it. Going live was something that I always wanted to do, but I was just scared. She listened to the poems I planned to recite before, during, and after the event. She was supportive and encouraging.

You need genuine, sweet, and consistent people in your life. Life is difficult enough without constantly having to deal with sour patch kids. You are driven, kind, resilient, and intelligent. There are so many things you can do on your own, but you still need your support system. You need your mom, your dad, and your sisters to hold you down. You need Grandma, aunties, brothers, cousins, uncles, or whoever it is to whom you look when you need a hand or a hug. Those are the people who pour into you, so your cup doesn't go empty. When life gets hectic, it's so important to have people who listen to you and encourage you.

I've gone through some painful situations. We all have. During those times, I always looked to God for help, but He gave me people here on Earth to help me too. I had friends who asked no questions; they just showed up. They were there for emergencies, heartbreaks, and funerals. They were there when I got the call for the interview and when I didn't get the job. They were always there to support, smile, laugh, make jokes, and encourage me that things would be okay. My support system kept me in their prayers, and I could tell. The reason I could tell they were praying for me wasn't only because I had them in my prayers, but also I could tell they were praying for me because the atmosphere was better when they were around. I could forget about the craziness of the world for a while. I would feel confident enough to keep pursuing goals after they seemed unattainable. My People Who Pour are my family who shifted to best friends, my best friends who are simultaneously my sisters, and my close friends who are only one call away.

Your friendships need to have authenticity and longevity. When longevity is not possible, authenticity is priceless. You need to know that your friends are for you. This is why family often makes the best friends. Your family has known you for all your life. Family always has your back. They are not fake friends or frenemies. You don't have to question their motives. Now, of course, we all have some family members who we can't trust with certain things, but we still know their love is real.

I've been blessed to have a best friend for 23 years. Naturally, we both have changed some since the 3rd grade, but we are consistently there for each other. Being there for her is the authenticity. Making time for me is the way she shows her authenticity. It doesn't matter how long you are friends if you don't show up when it matters. Friendships don't always last this long, which is why I feel deeply honored that our friendship has lasted. The longevity of friendship adds value because you have been through so much together. The authenticity of friendship is priceless because you have someone who will always show up for you.

Time doesn't necessarily define how much someone means to you. This is why I said authenticity is priceless when longevity isn't possible. You may have a really caring friend who you just met at the gym or in your neighborhood. Many of us have heard the saying, "You can meet somebody tomorrow who has better intentions for you than someone you've known forever." You don't have to be friends for a long time to know that you will be friends for a lifetime. As long as you have friends and/or family who you know are lifting you up and holding you down, you are in good hands.

You are always in God's hands, and He has a funny way of placing people strategically in your life. Your mentor, counselor, or therapist can be one of the people who pour into you. Their roles are different from a friend's role, but they play a huge role in renewing your confidence. They are in your support system. You have what you need in a support system when you have more than one person to whom you can go if you are feeling discouraged. You have a team of people who can bring joy back to you. They are loved ones who know who you are, and they can remind you of who you are when you forget. Those who support you are "*The People Who Pour.*"

Your people who pour are friends who don't make you feel judged when you're dealing with your mistakes. This doesn't mean they let you skate over them. They just support and advise you in a way that makes you feel like you can recover from the situation. As a woman, you encounter so many changes, plateaus, and elevations. You need support from the ones you love in the same way that you give support to them. You may choose them. They may choose you, or God may choose these people for you. They are the shoulders you didn't ask to cry on and the arms you didn't ask to hold you, but they are the ones who always are rooting for your success. They are "The People Who Pour" and you need them in your life.

I would not be where I am today without my support system. My family and friends truly have held me down in ways that I would have never imagined. I know we all have issues with our families at times, but let me tell you, there is no love like the love of family. I remember one time my baby cousin had to sit me down and tell me to relax when I was extremely stressed. First of all, how many people have the authority in your life to sit you down? It's a blessing to have someone to whom you actually listen, and she has the influence to make you sit down when she tells you to sit down. If you think about it, the people who are closest to you may work your nerves sometimes, but they love you endlessly. Your people who pour have your best interests at heart. Your family and friends see your value and your potential. They uplift and encourage you. I encourage you to not only thank the people who pour into you, but also I encourage you to hold on tightly to them. Go to them even when you feel ashamed because they will remind you that there is no need to be.

CHAPTER 10

I SAID WHAT I SAID

Sometimes you make the right decision. Sometimes you make the decision right. - Dr. Phil McGraw

Have you ever watched that show, *House in a Hurry*? It's about couples who have three days to purchase a home in another city. If you have ever been in the home buying process, you know how long it takes to find and purchase a home; I can guarantee you, 3 days ain't it. If you haven't purchased a home, just imagine buying your dream home. Think about the price you want to pay and the number of floors you'll want to have. Since you obviously cannot build it from the ground up in a hurry, think about all the beautiful details the house must have in order for you to buy it. Home buying is a lot of pressure, and that's without being on a 72-hour time clock. I was not on this show, but I felt like I was on the show during the summer of 2020 when I searched for a home. I felt like I was on an episode of *House in a Hurry:Pandemic Edition.*

A global pandemic changed everything for everybody. There was so much loss and tragedy but there were blessings as well. One of those blessings of the pandemic was low interest rates on homes. Low interest rates were a blessing and a curse because everybody and their momma's momma was out trying to purchase a home. I would go to view a house one day, and the house would be under contract the next day. I used to tell my friends, "I feel like the under contract ghost is following me." It was tough because I didn't even have the support I would normally have with me due to the pandemic. My family couldn't be there during the process. I had a specific time frame in which I needed to move. I had a limited budget as a single woman. I also had a vision of the home I always wanted to get, and it was hard fitting all of those things into one plan. I had to determine my non-negotiables. For me, the main thing was location and budget. The funny thing is that I ended up having to be a little flexible there too. I remember looking at two homes in a neighborhood. I said if one didn't work out, I was going to get the other home. I was making a lot of decisions at once. I was starting a new job, figuring out my finances, and trying to figure out how I was going to move.

I remember my mom asked if I was sure that I should be starting a new job and buying a home. I didn't know how to not be sure about the new job. It wasn't like I could renege. I had already accepted the position. I told her I was comfortable at my old job, but I felt like I needed a change. I knew what to tell her about the house, because buying a home was my dream. At times, it just felt like a mini-nightmare because of the pandemic, but it turned out great! My new job was different in a lot of ways. Some of the differences were good, and some of the differences I didn't like. At times, it was a struggle adjusting to the changes. Some of my old coworkers would say to me, "I bet you wished you had stayed over here." This was the most irritating statement that anyone could have ever said to me. I thought, *No, I don't wish I would have stayed there because I would never know what it was like over here. In fact, I don't really know what it's like over there anymore because a lot has changed since the pandemic.*

I think making decisions is scary because you feel like you can't go back after you make them. They seem so permanent and feel like something someone can hold over your head. There is a blessing in making a choice on your own. You get to say, "I did that!" when it works out. I think we have to be more confident that our decisions will work out in our favor. You should begin to look at your decisions and believe that what you decided was good enough. You are capable of making sound decisions. Feeling like you are unable to go back on your decisions is a little tricky because technically, you can.

You have the right to change your mind. Sometimes, you will need to change your mind; however, I would say a better way to "go back" is to simply adjust. Make a decision and stick to it. If part of your plan doesn't work out, pivot and make it happen, so your overall plan still takes place. For example, when I was in the process of buying my home, it seemed like I never was going to find anything that worked for me. I didn't let that stop me. I didn't look at homes that matched my family's preferences but fell short of what I wanted. I stuck to the type of location I wanted. I saved some money, so I could be a competitive buyer when it came to closing costs. I made a decision to move, and all I had to do was figure out what I was willing to live with and live without. It wasn't easy, but I stuck with it.

When things get shaky, don't change your mind about what you have decided. Yes, there are times when you need to jump ship, but that time is not when you first get on the ship. People say things like, "Don't rock the boat" and "Just stay where you are." I challenge you to ask them, "Is that what you did?" If their answer is yes, congratulate them on how that worked out for them, but you should know that you are not them. We are all individuals, and we have to make individual decisions. Stick to your decisions because after you weighed the options and evaluated what you wanted, you decided that this was what was best for you. Maybe, you decided at this point in your life, you needed something different. Change is scary for a lot of people, but how will you know what you like if you don't decide to take a chance on something new? How will you know where you'd like to be, if you don't explore new places?

Once you make a decision, you have to stick to it. If you keep going back and forth in your head, you literally will drive yourself crazy.

Speaking of crazy, I once went crazy over some couch pillows. I had a couch and was so excited when it came with two free decorative pillows. The pillows were gray and white. I did not like much about them except for the fact that they were free. I told myself that I would get one set of teal pillows to tie everything together. About three days later, I bought some teal pillows from the store and a half set of pillows from JCPenney, and I still wasn't satisfied. I called my sister and got her opinion about how things looked. She told me it wasn't quite right. I sent screenshots of other pillows I considered purchasing to my guy friend. When he and I Facetimed about the pillows, he said they weren't right either.

I was so frustrated, and I was doing the one thing I was trying to avoid. I was spending a hell of a lot of money on pillows. I didn't take any of them back at first. I held onto them in case a set I had worked out with a set I had not purchased yet. I also was afraid I wasn't going to find anything better. I checked a few more stores and Amazon, of course, and a couple weeks later, I had more pillows than couches. I called my guy friend all throughout the process of finding pillows, and he called me "*Indecisive Irene.*"

He was right. I was being indecisive, and I was okay with that because I usually am indecisive about a lot of things, or at least I was, until that point. I pretty much drove myself crazy looking for the perfect pillows and trying to get us all to agree on the same ones. I was trying to get the approval of two other people who did not even live in my home! It was madness. I was searching for everyone's input without realizing that their tastes were different from my taste. I should have stuck with what I said in the beginning and decided to purchase one set to tie everything together. I did not, so instead, I ended up with 4 sets of pillows and a possible. Now, I love all my pillows, and everything turned out well, but I really could have avoided some mess by just trusting myself.

Deep down, you know what you want; sometimes, you just don't think or believe it's possible. You know what you want, but you're just afraid to say it. You let other people bring it out of you instead of just outright saying, "This is what I want to do." My pillow talk may sound silly, but decorating my couch was obviously no joke to me. Furthermore, it allowed me to evaluate my decision making skills. I can't keep going back and forth in my mind and arguing with other people about the decisions I've already made. I have to make a choice and stick to it.

I always knew I wanted a lot of pillows, but initially, I wasn't willing to spend the time or money on them. I kind of went about the process the wrong way. Sometimes, the sacrifice that it takes for you to make a decision is more than you are willing to make. In every decision, you make a sacrifice. It's important for you to realize that and stick to your decisions. Your choices should be emphatic. You said what you said. Choose to stand by the decisions you make because in doing so, you begin to build your confidence about your decision making.

Decision making is scary. This is especially true when it comes to new experiences like finding love, buying homes, and raising children. Nevertheless, it is a fear we must face, and we must try to face it fearlessly. I'm so glad that I've gone through a phase in which I realized my indecisiveness was causing more harm than good. The case of the couch pillows helped me to grow as a woman. The experience helped me to realize that it was time to stop making myself crazy by continuously going back and forth on my decisions. I had to stop and trust my judgement. I had to think about what I wanted and what was best for me. Everyone won't always agree with your decisions, but they don't have to agree. They are not living your life. Be confident in your path. Don't turn back when things become a little more difficult than what you imagined. Stick to your decisions. Believe that the decision you made was the right one for you. Know that even if you make a wrong choice, Romans 8:28 says "*And we know that all things work together for good to those who love God, to those who are the called according to His purpose.*" Trust yourself and know that you are capable of making good decisions.

Chapter 11

Who Do You Hear?

"Good instincts usually tell you what to do before your head has figured it out."
– E. Michael Burke

Dating after the 99 and 2000s is kind of like the dial up internet speeds we used to have to deal with; it is terrible. It's super annoying, moves really slow, and takes a long time to get a connection. It's not impossible, but you just wish it was better. It's hard to figure out the things you can and should deal with when you are dating in today's society. So much has changed, yet many people still play those same games that they did when we were young. I never would have thought that the "talking" stage we used to do in middle school would still be happening 15 years later. I'm not against "talking." I just want to be able to move past that stage.

When I was dating different guys, so much was wrong. I always put my best foot forward, but I felt like I wasn't getting the same in return. I knew how I felt about each guy, but sometimes, I wanted it to be different. I wanted to feel less, or I wanted them to have more feelings for me. I would talk to my girls about what was happening, and I asked for their advice on the situation. One time, I dated a guy who was a pure gentleman. He opened every door and called me on the phone, but there was no chemistry. Our conversations did not leave me wanting more. He was so sweet, but it just wasn't working. I talked with my girls about it, and they said, "He's sweet. Maybe, you should give it more time." I wanted to say no, but I felt guilty for not liking him. So often, women complain about there not being any good men, and I had one right in front of me, but he wasn't right for me.

I've often asked others for relationship advice. I needed another woman's perspective on how much I should tolerate from a guy. How much was too much? I would ask my guy friends for their input as well. However, nobody truly can tell me what I should tolerate. Soon, I realized I needed to limit how much input I was getting from others. I had to limit that input before it unintentionally put me in places I didn't need to be. People always say, "As long as the good outweighs the bad." However, your threshold for what is "bad" might be different than someone else's threshold. You have to figure out what kind of bad you are willing to deal with or accept. The good may outweigh the bad, but if the "bad" is inconsistency, that may be too much for you. I was in a relationship where the good outweighed the bad, but the heaviness of the insecurity was too much for me. The good seemed to outweigh the bad, but really, I was in a cycle I didn't know how to break.

You have a little voice inside your head that helps you to read, think, and process information. That voice knows the answers to the questions you ask your friends. That voice knows what's best for you. That voice is your voice. It is imperative that this little voice has the ability to grow and be heard, especially when it comes to decision making. It's okay to seek advice and gather input from trusted friends and family. However, if all of your input is coming from others, then none of what you say or do will be of you. If you are receiving too much input when you are trying to make a decision, that little voice you have gets drowned out, and the thoughts of those around you are the ones that actually influence the decisions you make.

I had to make a decision to write this book. I had very limited input when I made this decision. There were two people I talked to about my decision, one on purpose, and one I told by accident. When I talked to my two friends about writing this book, they thought it was a good idea. One friend, however, wasn't sure about the process, and the other friend didn't think that it was the right time for me to write the book. I was extremely busy with work and still was adjusting to my move. They encouraged me to do it, but they didn't actually say, "Do it." I wanted to ask a couple of other people about it, but I knew their answer would be no, or they just would not be helpful. I wasn't looking for somebody to side with me, but I wasn't looking for anyone to be negative either. The book was big. It was going to be a little piece of my heart, open for the world to see.

Making the decision to write this book was something I immediately realized I had to do on my own. If I got too much input, all the other voices would smother mine. I had to learn how to listen to my inner voice. In some ways, I had to relearn how to do that. I had grown so accustomed to getting others' input on the things I planned to do in my life. I prayed that God would lead me and help me to see if this was something He wanted me to do. You know how God does after prayer. Mostly, it's silence that you get. Then, one night, I felt like God told me it was time. I was super scared, but I moved forward. I listened to myself and made a decision that made me happy.

I'm starting to trust my own voice more than anyone else's. That small voice is always with me and it always will be with me. You too have a voice. Can you hear it? Do you allow yourself time and space to listen to your inner voice? You have a voice and a say in your life. Things don't just happen to you. You make things happen in your life. When you use your voice, you are in more control of what happens to you. It's beneficial to get input from others. Some of our best decisions are made by listening to those who are wiser than us. Make sure, though, that your voice has the final say. Remember, it is your input that matters the most. We usually seek advice not just because we are unsure, but because we are not confident. We are afraid of making the wrong decision. In Chapter 6, we discussed how you have to be okay with the possibility of making a mistake. We learn and grow from our mistakes. Through God's grace, we move past the disappointment and hurt that comes from them. When you limit the amount of input you receive and listen to your own voice, you find confidence in knowing that the path you are on was chosen specifically by you.

No one can tell you what is right for you. People can advise you, but they cannot tell you, without a disclaimer, that the advice they give you truly is going to work. We give advice based on our experiences, but we all have different experiences. Sometimes, even if we have the same experience, we have different feelings about it because we are different people. This is why you must listen to your own voice. Don't second guess yourself. Try not to rely on others to tell you what you should tolerate. You know how you feel, and you know what you desire. Don't be afraid of saying it. Don't feel guilty about what you want. Don't feel guilty for wanting something different than everybody else.

There were times when I would be about to say something to someone, and I would hear my mother's voice. I would hear her voice in my head telling me what to say, but sometimes, I wished I heard myself instead. I wish my response was more immediate. I trust my mother, but I needed to trust myself. Years of going to others caused me to lose trust in my inner voice. I don't want you to experience that. I want you to hear you. I want you to listen to your own voice. I want you to know that your voice matters. It matters more than anyone else's voice. Your voice is strong when you allow it to be.

Chapter 12

Love is Patient

"Love is patient, love is kind. It does not envy, it does not boast, it is not proud. It does not dishonor others, it is not self-seeking, it is not easily angered, it keeps no record of wrongs. Love does not delight in evil but rejoices with the truth. It always protects, always trusts, always hopes, always perseveres. Love never fails." 1 Corinthians 13:4-8 NIV

If you asked me five years ago what I was looking for in a man, my first response would be, "He gotta be fine." However, fineness is not a fruit. It does not indicate how sweet a person's insides are. In fact, many times I found that the ones who looked fine on the outside were really jacked up on the inside. It happens, and while this is not true about everybody, it is true for many individuals. People get caught up in how attractive they are, and they treat others terribly because they know someone is always going to be checking for them. In their minds, someone is always going to think they look good, so there is no need for them to stress about you. The problem is at some point, that gets old. No one likes being dismissed or feeling like they can be replaced easily. You grow up and become a woman who wants more from a man. You don't want him to just look good, you want him to actually be good!

I feel like we all go through that phase though when we date for the wrong reasons. We tolerate crappy behavior because "He's fine." Sometimes, we do it because we feel like the connection is so deep. I think if the connection was that deep, he would treat you better. I was in a relationship in which I put my all in it. I sacrificed often, loved him deeply, and was extremely giving. The relationship just wasn't right. It was like pouring my love down an empty drain; he just couldn't hold it. No matter how much I gave, he always required more, yet he never gave much in return. I was willing to compromise and make changes, but he really wasn't willing to do the same for me. There were insecurity issues. His expectations were skewed, and we did too much fighting. The relationship ended, and eventually, I ended up being okay with him not being the one for me.

Sometimes, you really don't know until you know. You spend months, maybe even years, trying to figure out if you made the right decision. It takes time and patience to come to terms with how your life is going because of the decisions that others made for you. Others make decisions that affect your life, and you have to make your next move from there. It could be the decision someone made to lie to you, cheat on you, break up with you, or even pursue you. You have to take the next step and decide how you are going to respond to their decisions.

You may not know right away if the response you make is the right one. There's not always one single event or indicator that tells you you did the right thing. It could be after a series of events, or it could be a feeling of peace you get in a moment that lets you know you made the right choice. This is why you have to be patient. Give yourself time and grace to get your life situated. When my relationship ended, I struggled with it. Even though the situation was bad, I still wasn't sure if I made the right decision.

I started ignoring the bad things we had experienced, and I clung to the good memories we had. I was feeling like maybe, I made a mistake. After a few weeks, I could see the situation more clearly. As time progressed, I learned more and more about how I was delivered from that relationship. They say hindsight is 20/20. In the moments when I was going through that relationship, I thought I was fighting for something. I thought that all of my work was for us to work towards a future together. I just knew I was building with someone. I was wrong, and I didn't know it yet.

Several months later, the relationship was over. The future I envisioned was changing. It took time for me to be okay with that. Your vision changes when you have patience. I had to wait and go through the difficulties of that relationship in order to figure out it was meant to end. Forgive yourself for not leaving when you first saw the red flags. You were waiting patiently to see how everything would play out. You were being patient, hopeful, and kind. You gave it a chance, and it ended when it was the right time for you.

When I was dating a guy who tried to rush me into marriage, I used to tell him, "Why rush what you want to last forever?" Love is patient because real love takes time. It takes time to get to know someone and figure out how you all work together as a couple. It takes time to get to know people and figure out who they really are. One time, I dated a guy who was fineee, but he was not fine for very long. He lived kind of far from me, but I never could tell the distance. We talked often. He was consistent with his communication, and we had good chemistry. Then, we had a couple of instances when he started acting differently. He was being rude, and I wasn't used to that from him. For a little while, I tried to resolve the situation with him, but I realized I was holding on to someone who was letting go of me. I also was holding on to a situation that probably wasn't going to work anyway. We really lived too far apart. My girlfriends told me to stop tripping about someone who was so far away and who wasn't being very respectful towards me. I love that I have friends who help me take off my blinders when I need it. They are patient with me and protective of me. The same love they have for me is the love I want to have in my relationship one day. I realize that many times, the same advice they give me is the advice I would give them if the situation was reversed. It's funny how we love our friends enough to give them the advice we won't take ourselves. We want the best for our friends, but we accept less than that for ourselves.

Love is kind. I fell into a pattern in which I wasn't expecting situations to work out. It was easy to deal with guys who weren't giving me much because I was used to it. I was used to being disappointed. Disappointment is not key. You don't have to keep dealing with guys who are not pouring into you because you are not used to experiencing that. Just because you've dealt with men who were inconsistent and immature doesn't mean you have to continue to put up with that. Get back to your standards. Better yet, you should raise your standards. You are golden! You give love, so you should expect to receive it. You should place yourself around people and in situations in which you will be treated with love and respect. When you notice someone not valuing who you are or what you give, you should try to back away from him or her.

Sometimes, we begin to make repetitive bad decisions because we are used to them. We are used to dealing with the outcomes of them. You are better than your worst mistake. You are capable of moving past bad decisions. Everyday, strive to love yourself enough to know that you deserve better. Be patient enough to wait for better. The best love you can have is the love you have for yourself. It is a love you work on each day that will continue to grow as you remain patient, trust God, and trust everything He has put in you.

Be okay with waiting. Rome was not built in a day, and love is not made in a minute. This includes the love you have for yourself. We are often our own worst critics. Take time to get to know who you are and accept every part of you. Accept your bad and your good. Love yourself each day in spite of your flaws. Be generous with the love you have for yourself, so when it is time for you to find love, you know who is good for you and who is not. Wait to see who is adding love to you and who is taking love away from you. Give people time to show themselves to you. I know it's hard to wait when it seems like everyone else has something you don't. However, you are building a foundation.

You are developing into the type of woman who knows how to give love, recognize B.S., and receive love too. That development takes time. It takes highs and lows. Be patient while you are waiting for love and be consistent in the love you are showing yourself. Don't settle. There is one thing you cannot afford to lose and that is the love you have for yourself.

EPILOGUE

Now that you have completed *Girl, You Are Golden: 12 Lessons about Love, God, and Relationships*, expect to value yourself in a whole new way. After reading this book, you will be more self-confident. You will know how to take care of yourself. This book reminds you that you should come first in your own life. You will feel empowered to love God and rely on Him. You will be more confident about the standards that you have for your relationships. This book has given you the tools to love and trust yourself.

Hopefully, you took your time in reading this book but don't take too much time implementing what it taught you. Don't waste another minute doubting yourself or being too hard on yourself. Take time to take care of yourself. Spend time with God, so you can love yourself a little better and more each day. When you love yourself more, you stop accepting less than what you deserve. When you trust yourself, you feel confident about your decisions.

You don't have to keep going back and forth in your head about your next steps.

Some of the main concepts I shared in *Girl, You Are Golden: 12 Lessons about Love, God, and Relationships* are about trusting and loving yourself, taking care of yourself, and loving God.

- ✓ Chapter 1 *Who Has Your Heart?* is a chapter that reflects on how important your relationship with God is when you are dating or in a relationship.
- ✓ Chapter 2 *Address the Stress* is a chapter about the importance of therapy and addressing the stress in your life.
- ✓ Chapter 3 *Is God on the Calendar*? is a chapter about how we prioritize our relationship with God and spend time with Him.
- ✓ Chapter 4 *Select All That Apply* is a chapter about making your own choices and being confident in them.
- ✓ Chapter 5 *Goal-Getter* is a chapter about pursuing goals in spite of the obstacles that you face.
- ✓ Chapter 6 *What if You Fumble?* talks about being okay with the possibility of making mistakes.
- ✓ Chapter 7 *Shine Like the Sun* discusses the importance of feeling beautiful, putting yourself first, and practicing self-care.

- ✓ Chapter 8 *Who Else Can You Be?* is a chapter that focuses on not allowing others to make you feel bad about who you are.
- ✓ Chapter 9 *The People Who Pour* is a chapter about your support system and the vital role they play in your life.
- ✓ Chapter 10 *I Said What I Said* is a chapter about sticking to your decisions.
- ✓ Chapter 11 *Who Do You Hear?* talks about trusting your judgement and listening to your inner voice when you are making decisions.
- ✓ Chapter 12 *Love is Patient* is the final chapter, which talks about having patience with love and loving yourself. It discusses how time and patience will help you to see things more clearly.

This is the time for you to let go of the past and love who you are! Love that you are becoming a woman who truly knows, loves, and trusts herself. You may have taken on too much in the past, or you may have been disappointed in the way you handled certain situations, but those moments are gone.

You have overcome old hurts, heartaches, and hasty decisions. Girl, You Are Golden! You glitter from the inside out. You were already exceptional before, and now, you just have a better understanding of how magical you are.